THE NO-NONSENSE KEY

Read the NO-NONSENSE FINANCIAL GUIDE TO UNDERSTANDING MONEY MARKET FUNDS

- if you want your extra cash secure and easily accessible
- if you want your extra cash to work for you
- if you want a high yield investment

No-Nonsense Financial Guide to Understanding Money Market Funds

ARNOLD CORRIGAN and PHYLLIS C. KAUFMAN

LONGMEADOW PRESS

To E. Y. ("YIP") HARBURG—
"Thanks for a glorious time"

The NO-NONSENSE FINANCIAL GUIDE Series was designed and produced exclusively for, and is published exclusively by, Longmeadow Press, an imprint of Waldenbooks®. For information address: Waldenbooks Co., Inc., 201 High Ridge Rd., Stamford, Connecticut 06904.

ISBN: 0-681-29915-0

Production services: W. S. Konecky Associates
Text and cover design: Adrian Taylor

Printed in the United States of America

CONTENTS

PREFACE

Your financial security and that of your family depend on making the most of your money now. With as little as $250 or $500 to invest, the NO-NONSENSE FINANCIAL GUIDES will introduce you, step by step, into the world of finance.

The NO-NONSENSE FINANCIAL GUIDES put you in control.

The NO-NONSENSE FINANCIAL GUIDES take the fear out of finance.

Geared toward your financial goals, each easy-to-follow book in the NO-NONSENSE series introduces you into a different part of the world of investment opportunity.

Read several NO-NONSENSE FINANCIAL GUIDES before you invest. The short time it takes you to read and understand a NO-NONSENSE FINANCIAL GUIDE is your first step toward a secure future.

Chapter One

Introduction: Who Should Read the NO-NONSENSE FINANCIAL GUIDE TO UNDERSTANDING MONEY MARKET FUNDS?

Money market funds are a subject that everyone should know about, not only because many people will *use* money market funds—for handling cash, and perhaps for longer-term investment; but also because, in a remarkably short time, money market funds have become an important part of the whole American economic structure. If you want to understand the whole financial scene, and how you can make your own investment plans fit into it profitably, you need to understand what money market funds are and how they work.

A money market fund isn't a bank. But from the standpoint of you, the customer, a money market fund, often called simply a "money fund," has many of the characteristics of a bank. When you put your money in, you expect it to be perfectly safe and easily available. And you expect it to earn a good interest rate—the highest rate consistent with safety.

Still, some people don't trust money market funds, because they aren't banks. But other people remember how money market funds came into prominence in the 1970s by paying much higher rates of interest than banks. Many of these people like money funds *because* they aren't banks.

Before we discuss just what money market funds *are*, and what they can do for you, let's give ourselves a framework by talking very briefly about your own financial needs and objectives.

1

Chapter Two

Cash Management

"Cash management" has become a common phrase in business today. With interest and inflation rates generally higher than they were years ago, it is now more important than ever to earn interest on every dollar every day possible. And with the speed of financial transactions increasing, the ability to move money in and out of deposit cost-effectively and efficiently, with the least possible trouble and loss of time, is essential.

Individuals don't feel these problems quite so keenly as businesses. But the problems are there just the same. Whatever your longer-term investments may be, you need to be aware of cash management and to have a certain amount of your money perfectly safe and quickly and easily available. Of course, the higher the interest rate you earn on this cash, the better off you will be.

To sum it up in the language of the investment professionals, your cash management objectives are:

Safety: You want to be sure that your dollars are held safely for you without any risk.

Liquidity: You want those dollars to be convertible into cash whenever you wish.

Convenience: You want just that. (Later on, we'll talk about some of the specific conveniences available to you.)

High Yield: You want to earn as much interest on your money as possible, without getting in the way of your other objectives.

Millions of people (and businesses) use money market funds for cash management that meets these objectives. But for many people the funds also meet another objective. This other objective isn't always clearly distinguished, but it can be just as important.

Chapter Three

Investment Management

What is investment management? It relates to the money that people *don't* need to have instantly available—the money that they invest for the longer term in some form that they feel will best meet their future financial needs and objectives.

Risk and Reward

Investing always involves a trade-off between *risk* and *reward*. The higher the reward you aim for, the greater the risks and uncertainties are likely to be. For example, if you buy a few ounces of gold because you think the price of gold is going to rise, you have bought an investment that is risky even for the best experts. If your timing is right, your money could indeed double or triple in the course of a few years. If you are wrong, you may lose money. (That's the risk.) In either case, you are sure to see the price of gold zig-zag, sometimes violently, and the value of your investment may change sharply from day to day. (That's the uncertainty.)

Of course, there are other investments with less volatility than gold. Common stocks, for example, are a much more practical long-term ("growth") investment, and there are ways of investing in common stocks that make the risks and uncertainties much less extreme than in the case of gold.

But in personal investing, some people find almost any degree of uncertainty deeply uncomfortable. They want safety and certainty, and are perfectly willing to put aside thoughts of rapid growth for their investment dollars in order to achieve peace of mind.

Years ago, people who wanted complete safety for their investment dollars often were content to leave their savings in a bank of some sort and to accept whatever rate of interest the bank paid. If they didn't need to spend the interest every year, they left it in the bank so that their money would grow. Many people still use banks in this way. They may choose carefully among the various types of accounts and certificates their bank offers, in order to earn the highest possible rates of interest. Or, in some cases, out of habit or inertia, they may leave their money in old-style passbook accounts that earn relatively low rates.

Other people who want this complete safety have turned to money market funds. In succeeding chapters we will describe how the money funds invaded the territory that traditionally had been held by banks, and we will discuss the advantages and disadvantages of money funds, particularly in comparison to banks. For now, we want to make the point that a money market fund can serve two separate functions. First, it can provide *cash management* for handling money that you are using currently or that you expect to need in the not-too-distant future. And second, it can give you *investment management* in the form of complete safety plus interest earnings for your long-term investment dollars.

The two functions aren't the same, and we may find that a money market fund is better for you for one purpose than it is for another. Obviously, the answers are important for your financial planning. But first, we need to examine more specifically just what a money market fund is and how it functions.

Chapter Four

What Is a Money Market Fund?

A money market fund is a particular type of mutual fund. A mutual fund is an organization in which money from thousands of investors, large and small, is pooled into a large single unit for investment under the management of skilled professionals.

What distinguishes a money market fund from other mutual funds of varying purposes is just how this pool of money is invested. In a money fund, investments are geared toward the maximum in safety and liquidity. This is accomplished by investing in the "money market"—an incredibly large marketplace where hundreds of billions of dollars are regularly lent on a short-term basis among governments, banks, corporations and other institutions. The loans may run for as little as one day and rarely for more than a year. The goal of a money market fund is to earn as much as it reasonably can for its shareholders by investing their money in the safest of these loans.

Because a money fund is large (anywhere up to several billion dollars), it enjoys many advantages that would not be possible for single investors acting alone. It can afford to hire the best professional managers and research advisers. It can diversify, that is, spread its investments over a large number of individual securities, so that a mistake in one or two choices will not have a significant impact on the fund's total performance. By buying or selling in large quantities, it can often get better prices than are available on small transactions. And for those trades (purchases or sales) where the fund pays a commission, the commissions are relatively at much lower rates than would be paid by a small investor.

A Bit of History
Although the money market funds are now the best-known type of mutual fund—and in recent years they have held more investor dollars than all other types of mutual funds combined—it wasn't always that way. Before 1972, there wasn't even such a fund as a money market fund. There were some mutual funds that invested their shareholders' money in common stocks, and a smaller number that invested in bonds, and some that invested in a combination of stocks and bonds. That was about it.

Then some far-sighted individuals conceived the idea of a new type of mutual fund that would, in effect, compete with the banks. In the late 1970s, these new funds began to grow at a spectacular rate. Interest rates were rising sharply both on long-term bonds (which represent long-term loans) and in the short-term money market. But most small bank depositors were still receiving from 5% to 6% maximum on their money, tied down by antiquated governmental banking regulations.

The money market funds, by contrast, were investing their shareholders' money in the relatively unfettered money market. They were earning interest at high "market" rates—the rates being paid by governments, banks and corporations on short-term borrowings—and were able to pass these rates on to their shareholders less a relatively small amount to cover the funds' expenses.

As between the money funds and the banks, it was not a close contest. In 1981, when interest rates reached a peak, many money funds earned better than 17% (yes, 17%) for their shareholders. By 1982, the money funds were managing over $200 billion of shareholders' money—a good part of it taken away from the banks.

The Reawakening of the Banks

But the banks fought back. For years, the banks had been happy to see the government help their profits by putting a ceiling on the interest rates they were allowed to pay to depositors. Now the banks and their government regulators realized that a new competitor had emerged and that the old approach no longer worked.

At first, the banks tried for legislation that would have curtailed the operations of the money funds. Since banks wield strong political influence, it seemed at times that they might succeed. But the money funds had already grown too popular, and too many people felt that they had a personal stake in seeing the money funds continue to flourish. Piece by piece, the legislation died away.

The only course left to the banks was to compete with the money funds and to give their depositors a better break. Banks had always been allowed to pay high interest rates on "certificates of deposit" (deposits for a fixed time period) of $100,000 or more. In the late 1970s a breakthrough was made when the banks were allowed to offer six-month certificates of deposit ("CDs") in denominations of $10,000 or more at interest rates tied to the rate on Treasury bills. (The Treasury bill interest rate is the *market rate* paid by the U.S. Treasury on short-term borrowings.) Step by step, banking regulations were expanded and the banks were permitted to offer new types of accounts and new types of certificates paying interest rates at or close to the market rate.

The Differences Narrow

Finally, in December 1982, banks were permitted to begin offering "money market deposit accounts"—generally referred to simply as money market accounts or market rate accounts. These accounts compete directly and effectively with the money market funds. Unlike CDs, the money market accounts have no maturity date—money can be moved in and out at any time and in whatever minimums the bank permits. The bank fixes the rate it will pay on a weekly basis. However, whenever the balance in a market rate account drops below $2,500, the account stops earning the money market rate and earns the low passbook interest rate instead.

No, this is not a book about banks. But the banks and the money market funds have become such close competitors that from the investor's standpoint, it is impossible to talk intelligently about one without also considering the other. The money funds skyrocketed to prominence partly on their own merits, and partly because of bank shortcomings. Now it's a closer race.

How a Money Fund Works

In underlying structure, bank money market accounts and money funds are not so similar. A bank takes in money from depositors—some of whom primarily want interest, while others may primarily want service—and lends the money out in many different ways, including some loans that may be relatively risky. Out of the interest the bank *receives* by lending, it *pays* interest to its depositors at whatever rates it finds necessary, based on competition and legal limitations. Whatever is left over is used to pay expenses and, hopefully, provide a profit. The interest rate received by depositors may or may not reflect fairly the rates that the bank itself is earning.

A money market fund, being a mutual fund, provides a much more direct pass-through mechanism. The shareholders actually *own* the fund. When an investor puts money in, he or she is actually *purchasing* shares of stock in the fund. The fund earns what it can by investing the shareholders' money, pays its expenses, and passes on all the rest of its income to the shareholders.

There's no profit left at the end, but one of the fund's expenses is the investment advisory fee (or management fee) it pays to its investment adviser (or manager) for management of its investments

7

and business arrangements. This fee is likely to be about ½ of 1% annually of the fund's assets. So if the fund is $100 million in size, the annual fee to the manager may be $500,000.

In practice, the manager is usually the organization that sponsored and promoted the fund. The management fee they get is how they make *their* profit. If the fund grows very large, the fees can become very profitable to the manager. But as a percentage of your investment, the fee is quite modest, and, if the manager is doing a good job, there's no reason for you to worry about it.

Other expenses may take an additional ½ of 1%—payments to an agent for maintaining shareholder records and processing shareholder transactions, fees to the custodian bank that holds the fund's investment documents in safekeeping, payments to printers, fees to lawyers and accountants, etc. So the fund's total expenses may amount annually to about 1% of assets. Actually, due to the economies of scale, many of the larger money funds have been able to keep expenses to a lower percentage—perhaps ¾ of 1% of assets.

What this means to the shareholders is simple. If a money fund can earn an average of 8% on its investments, it will probably pay between 7% and 7¼% to its shareholders. If it earns 10%, it will probably pay between 9% and 9¼%.

The concept developed and refined by the money market funds is really remarkably simple. The pass-through, as stated earlier, is direct. No marketing committee decides what interest rate will be paid to you. What the fund earns (less expenses) is what you get.

Chapter Five

Dividends

You may be surprised to hear payments to you described as "dividends." In a money fund, aren't you earning *interest*? There's no doubt that the fund is passing on to you the interest it earns on the short-term loans it makes. But since, in a money fund, you are not just a depositor, but actually a *shareholder* (a part owner of the fund), these earnings are technically termed *dividends* when they are passed on to you. It doesn't really make that much difference. People often talk about the "interest" they earn in their money fund because that's the way it feels and it's a clear and simple way of putting it. We will often state it that way too, but remember that technically, and for purposes of your tax return, you are receiving dividends.

At this point we had better say a word about how those interest earnings are passed on to you. A money fund usually "declares" dividends daily, which means that every day it calculates the fund's income for the day and the proportionate share due to each shareholder. Dividends may be *paid*—that is, actually entered by computer on the shareholder's account—either daily or monthly. From the shareholder's point of view, this doesn't really matter—either method gives the shareholder the effect of daily compounding, the most advantageous type of compounding for the shareholder. Some people like to have the dividends mailed to them monthly; others prefer to reinvest and let the dividends accumulate, taking the money out or letting it grow when and as they please.

One more technical item. Note that while money fund shares are priced at $1.00, the fund's accounting system deals in fractional shares to three decimal places. So when dividends are credited to your account, you get what you have earned down to the last penny. The same is true when you move money in or out of your account.

Chapter Six

Advantages of Money Market Funds

This chapter discusses the advantages of money market funds.

Of course, we've already described some of the key advantages. Investors first came flocking to the money funds because of the *high yield* the funds offered, and this certainly continues to be one of the key attractions of the funds. The yield that the average money fund earns for its shareholders is far higher than in traditional-type bank accounts; and it's only a shade lower than the rates earned by large institutions investing in the money market (the difference being the small amount subtracted to pay the money fund's operating expenses).

The next advantage is *safety*. We'll have more to say about the safety of the money funds in Chapter 11, where we make some comparisons between the money funds and the banks. For now, suffice it to say that the safety record of the money funds has been remarkable—about as close to perfect as anything gets in this world. While the value of a fund's shares could, in theory, drop from $1.00 per share to 99 cents, the possibility in the case of any well-established fund is so remote that we think you can forget about it.

The next advantage of the funds is *convenience*. Over the years the funds have concentrated on attracting shareholders by giving them good service, and a variety of services.

The first convenience is the *low starting minimums*. The required minimum to open a money fund account usually ranges between $2,500 and $1,000, but there are some funds with minimums of $500 or even lower. If your balance drops below this minimum for a certain period of time, the fund usually reserves the right to close out your account and send you a check. But as long as the account is open, any balance you have earns the full fund rate. There's no problem of seeing your yield cut because your balance has dropped below $2,500 or some other arbitrary figure.

There are a whole set of fund conveniences that tie in with the advantage of *liquidity*—the quickness and ease with which you can take money *out* of the fund. Generally you have several choices. Most money funds let you withdraw money (or, technically, redeem shares) simply by writing a *check*, which has become one of the most popular features offered by the funds. Each check must be for more than a certain minimum amount (typically $500 or sometimes $250), but usually there is no charge for the checks and no restriction on how many can be written. Your money continues to earn interest until the check clears at your fund's custodian bank. It's a fine "cash management" arrangement for writing larger checks and for making periodic transfers into your regular bank checking account. You should request the check-writing privilege when you open your money fund account, unless there's some very specific reason why you know you won't make use of it.

If you so indicate on your original order form, most money funds will also let you take money out (redeem shares) by *telephone*. You can have a check sent to your address—usually the custodian bank will be able to get a check in the mail within a day after your phone call. Or you can ask that money be *wired* directly to your bank for deposit in your bank account. This procedure gets the money transferred within several hours. There is usually a minimum on the amount that the fund will wire, and there may be a small charge for the service, but it is obviously useful if you are in a hurry. Please note that you can't have this service unless you indicate, on your original order form, the exact bank name and account number to which you will want to have money wired—the fund has to be careful that it doesn't accept fraudulent telephone instructions to have money wired to the wrong bank account. If you haven't requested the service on your original order form, you can file a separate authorization later with the custodian bank.

You can also wire money *in* for deposit to your fund account. This is important if you are making a large transfer of money from your bank to the fund and you want it to begin earning interest as soon as possible. Phone the fund office for instructions, and follow them carefully. Money sent by wire moves with great speed, but it happens quite commonly that the receiving bank can't figure out what account the money belongs to.

The fund will usually also provide that any instructions given by telephone can also be given by telegram, if you so request. This may be useful particularly if you want to have a written record of your instructions.

You can also redeem money from your fund in the traditional mutual fund way, by writing a letter. In a money fund, this is certainly the hard way to do it. Find out what the fund's rules are with respect to signature guarantees—your signature on the letter (or both signatures in the case of a joint account) may have to be guaranteed by a commercial bank or a brokerage firm. The guarantee simply confirms that the signer really is the person that he or she claims to be.

You will also probably need a signature guarantee on your letter whenever you change instructions on the account, for example by requesting the check-writing privilege when you haven't requested it before, or changing the name of the bank to which you want money wired. In cases like these, the fund obviously has to be careful that it isn't taking instructions from the wrong person, and you should consider the safety well worth the slight inconvenience involved in getting the signature guarantee. The fund has less reason to worry when it follows instructions simply to send a check payable to the registered owner(s) of the account at the address originally given on the application.

Most funds also offer some additional ways to take money out conveniently. We have already mentioned that you can arrange to have *dividends* mailed to you monthly, if you don't want to let them accumulate. Also, most funds offer *automatic withdrawal plans* under which you can have a check for a regular amount mailed to you monthly or quarterly. You can pick any amount you choose above a certain low minimum.

You will receive monthly or quarterly *statements* from the fund showing all transactions for the period. The statements are usually clear and simple, though they vary in style from fund to fund. Some funds also send you a confirmation after every transaction showing your new balance, while others don't. If you write checks against your fund account, some funds will send each cancelled check back to you after it clears (perhaps with a confirmation of the transaction, perhaps not), while others return the checks to you on a monthly basis. Be careful—some funds don't send the checks back at all, which is a poor policy from the standpoint of your tax records.

One of the most important service features is the ability to get quick answers from the fund when you have a question or when something seems to have gone wrong. Most funds recognize that one of the chief requirements for keeping shareholders happy is good telephone service, and they have toll-free "800" numbers that give you the current yield of the fund and put you through to people trained to help you and answer your questions. At least some funds succeed in giving very good service of this sort, and if you have started with a fund that you find falls short, don't hesitate to switch. A fund management that is smart (and most are) will also pressure its servicing bank to give good service, but you may find that the bank responds less efficiently to phone calls than the fund office.

Switching

There's one great advantage of the money market funds that might be termed a convenience but that is really far more basic. This is the ability to *switch* your money easily from the money fund to other investments and back again. If your money fund is part of a larger mutual fund group (a "family of funds"), you can easily make this type of switch to any of the other funds in the group, which may include common stock funds, bond funds, tax-exempt funds, etc. (see the NO-NONSENSE FINANCIAL GUIDE TO MUTUAL FUNDS). Usually the group will arrange to let you do this by a simple phone call. There may be a small processing charge for each switch, but it shouldn't be significant (see Chapter 14).

If your total financial planning is limited to a money market fund and a bank checking account, this ability to switch won't seem important to you. But if you are investing seriously for the long run, or even if you are introducing more variety into your investments for short-run purposes, switching can be a major advantage. One of the keys to any investment program, long-term or short-term, is *flexibility*—the ability to make changes easily and quickly when your needs or outside conditions change. It's easy to be lazy about making such changes, and to miss opportunities that you should have taken. In a mutual fund group, the switching privilege removes any excuse for laziness on your part, and encourages you to be a good, prompt, efficient manager of your own investments.

If the fund group is *no-load*, it means that fund shares are sold without any commission ("load"), and there are no special charges to consider except the possible small processing charge on the switches referred to above.

If the money fund is part of a *load* group, it means that most of the funds in the group are sold by brokers or salespersons *with* a commission (load)—even though the money fund itself will almost universally be no-load.* In this case, you will pay the load the first time you switch from the money fund to one of the load funds in the group. But once you have paid this price of admission

---

*In the early days of the money market funds, several were sold on a commission or "load" basis. Competition eliminated the loads, and now there are only a very few "load" money market funds still left. It goes without saying that you should avoid them.

to the group, you will probably be able to switch that portion of your money among the various funds for only the small processing fees on the transfers. And if you originally started with one of the load funds in the group rather than with the money fund, the same principle applies.

In a money fund sponsored by a brokerage firm, the fund obviously is intended to tie in with brokerage firm procedures so that your money is available for other investments. If you are not already dealing with an individual broker at the firm, the firm will be glad to assign one to you.

In discussing the advantages of switching, we are obviously suggesting that a money market fund, by itself, doesn't give you an adequate long-run investment program. We think that most people, even those who are most content with the money funds, should consider some of the many other available investments for their long-run financial planning. But if you were to have only one kind of long-run investment, a money fund certainly would not be the worst. In Chapter 17 we will have a little more to say about the ways in which money funds can fit into your long-run investment program.

There's one more advantage of the money market funds that isn't easy to see, but which we think is important. Because they are a type of mutual fund, the money market funds operate under the regulatory eye of the U.S. Securities and Exchange Commission (SEC). The regulation is strict. Bank regulators have sometimes been accused of being too lenient toward the banks they regulate, but the SEC has generally kept a firm hand on the mutual fund industry, and on money market funds in particular. In its accounting, its choice of investments, its portfolio valuation, its handling of shareholder transactions, its dividend computations, and countless other areas, a money fund must follow a host of careful, tight regulations.

The Goldfish Bowl
Moreover, money fund managers, like managers of other mutual funds, operate in a "goldfish bowl." As a money fund shareholder, quarterly or semi-annually you receive a full, detailed list of the fund's investments and a report on yield for the latest period. At least twice a year, the fund's reports must include full financial statements, showing exactly what income the fund received, what its expenses were (broken down by category), and what net income was left for the shareholders.

You know exactly how much money the management organization is paid for running the fund, and the management knows that its policies and performance are spread out fully on the public record and can easily be compared with the competition. In fact, if your fund is earning well relative to comparable funds and is giving you good service, you may wonder why so much detailed disclosure information is sent to you. But it's a comfort to know that it's all there when you want it. You may possibly look for excitement in your other investments, but your money market fund is truly intended to be worry-free.

Chapter Seven

Disadvantages of Money Market Funds

While a money market fund can do many things for you, there are some things it can't do, and some advantages it doesn't have.

Insurance
Some people feel that the big disadvantage of a money fund is that it carries no government guarantee—unlike banks, where every account is insured up to $100,000 by a government agency. In view of the safety record of the money funds, we are not convinced that this difference is terribly important. But it is a difference, and there are certainly many people to whom it matters.

Checking and Cash
While a money fund may feel like a bank in some respects, there are some banking functions that a money fund doesn't provide. Although you can use a money fund for paying your large checks, you can't use it for your regular day-to-day checking needs. More importantly, you can't walk into a money fund office in an emergency and get cash, as you can in a bank—the fund pays your money out to you only by check or wire, which you then have to take to your bank if you want cash. (We should note that some large money fund organizations are considering arrangements that would let you get cash from your money fund account through automatic teller machines. But it probably will be a while before you can count on this.)

Taking Money Out
When you put money in a money fund, it may take a while before you can draw it out. It is hard for a fund to know its shareholders as well as a bank knows its depositors, and the funds have been plagued by creative crooks who have tried to deposit bad checks with the fund and then draw the money out before the fund had a chance to discover that the checks were worthless. As a result, many of the funds now require you to wait two weeks or so before drawing out any money you have deposited, unless the deposit was by certified check or wire transfer. This can be inconvenient. We often complain that banks are unreasonably slow in clearing checks

that have been deposited; in this area a money fund is likely to be slower.

Freedom of Choice

In comparing money funds to banks, there's another point to note that may be important to your long-run planning. Many people, quite reasonably, value the simplicity of the funds compared with the confusing number and variety of accounts and certificates available through the average bank. And the "substantial penalty for early withdrawal" imposed on most bank certificates has passed into popular folklore as a symbol of frustration. But bank certificates do serve a purpose—in fact, two purposes.

First, if you are willing to tie up your money for a specific period, bank certificates ordinarily pay a higher rate of interest than is being paid at any given time on bank money market accounts, and usually higher than is being paid by money market funds as well.

Second, if you see a risk that interest rates are declining or may be about to decline, bank certificates let you lock in current rates for a given period and protect yourself against loss of yield. Of course, if interest rates then rise instead of decline, you may be sorry that you locked in a rate too soon; and you may wish that you had held your money in a money fund or bank money market account, where you would have benefited almost immediately from the new, higher rates. But your judgment is just as likely to turn out right, and in any case you have had the freedom to make your own decision. Obviously, bank certificates let you make certain decisions and provide a certain type of investment that you can't make in a money fund.

Later on, we'll return to the question of when a money fund may or may not be the best tool for your financial planning. But first we need to look at the types of money funds, how they differ and what they do.

Chapter Eight

Types of Money Market Funds

Money market funds can be divided into a few different categories.

Sponsors
One way of distinguishing among the funds is according to who sponsors them. We have already touched on some of the possibilities. There are money funds that are part of no-load mutual fund groups. There are some that are part of load mutual fund groups. There are some that are completely independent.

There are funds that are affiliated with brokerage firms. You will often see these listed in directories as "stockbroker-affiliated." These fall into two subcategories: funds maintained primarily for the brokerage firm's existing customers, and those open to the general public. We won't try to generalize about the former type. Of those open to the public, some are indistinguishable from any other money fund. Some have higher starting minimums, in several cases as high as $5,000 or $10,000, and some don't offer check-writing privileges. If you are looking for a money fund and there are brokerage offices conveniently near you, it can't hurt to walk in and ask what they have available for the general public. But be sure that the fund has the services you want before you decide to put your money in.

Some other types of institutions, including bank trust departments, have money funds that are offered only to their own clients. This is another type of fund on which we won't dwell, but this book should teach you enough about funds so that you will be able to tell whether a particular fund gives you the services and features you need and have a right to expect. Don't confuse this type of money fund with a completely different category, the group of money funds that may have any type of sponsor but that are made available primarily to institutions and other large investors. This particular type of fund may eliminate some of the services desired by individual investors in an attempt to reduce costs and produce the highest possible yield; starting minimums are generally high.

Types of Investment
We now turn to an even more important way of grouping money

market funds—according to the type of securities in which they invest.

Early in this book we stated that the money market funds earn interest on their shareholders' money by making the safest short-term loans to government entities, banks, and major corporations. This description accurately fits most of the money funds, which—for want of a better term—we will refer to as "regular" money market funds.

There is a second and smaller group of money funds that, for the very maximum in safety, lend *only* to the U.S. government and its agencies. There is a third group that lend *only* to state and local governments, for the specific reason that the interest paid by state and local governments is exempt from federal income taxes. Since this income retains the tax exemption when passed through to shareholders as dividends, this third group of funds is generally referred to as the "tax-exempt" or "tax-free" money market funds.

At the end of 1983, the regular money market funds were managing about $140 billion of assets for shareholders, the government-only money funds about $20 billion, and the tax-free money funds about $17 billion. So these funds in total were handling about $175 billion for investors of various types. That compared with about $115 billion in all other types of mutual funds combined. But the money fund assets are still dwarfed by the total of over $1 *trillion* ($1,000 billion) in savings and loan associations, savings banks, and credit unions combined—not to mention tremendous additional amounts held in savings accounts at commercial banks.

Now we will talk about how the money funds actually invest your money for maximum safety. But first a word of explanation.

Where Your Money Goes

We have stated that the regular funds invest by making short-term loans to government entities, banks, and corporations. But for those who don't know how the money market works, we hasten to point out that this does not involve negotiating individual loans with any of those borrowers. Mechanically, the way lenders invest in the money market is by *buying* "debt instruments"—traditionally, pieces of paper (nowadays, more likely, computer entries) that state that the borrower owes a certain amount to the rightful owner of the piece of paper, and this amount is due on a certain specific date together with interest at a specified rate.

The beauty of this arrangement, and of the money market as a whole, is that the vast majority of these debt instruments are "negotiable," meaning that they can be bought and sold freely. When a lending institution finds that it needs money back, it simply turns around and sells the debt instrument to another lender who on that day happens to have excess cash. So what makes these loans "liquid" is not only that the loans will be paid off within a very short time, but, even more important, that any individual lender can pull its money out at will (usually in less than 24 hours) through the money market mechanism.

What do the money funds buy? As of December 31, 1983, the $140 billion or so held by the "regular" money market funds were invested roughly as follows:

Type	% of Total
U.S. government debt (U.S. Treasury securities and securities of U.S. government agencies)	11%
Bank debt (certificates of deposit)	32
Bank-guaranteed debt (bankers' acceptances)	14
Corporate debt (commercial paper)	33
Repurchase agreements	9
Other	1
TOTAL	100%

U.S. Treasury Obligations

The type of government debt instrument most commonly bought by the money funds is *U.S. Treasury bills,* the short-term debt issued in tremendous quantities by the Treasury. The money funds may occasionally also buy Treasury *notes* (intermediate-term) or *bonds* (long-term) if these happen to be very close to their "maturity date"—the date when they are paid off. And the funds may buy debt of such government agencies as the Federal National Mortgage Association, Federal Home Loan Bank, etc., which generally pay slightly higher interest rates than direct Treasury obligations.

Bank Obligations

The bank debt consists mainly of certificates of deposit (CDs), in large denominations, issued by commercial banks—one of the prime ways by which the banks raise money for their own lending operations. These include "Eurodollar CDs," which are certificates of deposit issued by foreign branches of U.S. banks in dollar denominations. Also included are a smaller amount of CDs issued by savings and loans and other banking institutions.

"Bankers' acceptances" are short-term commercial debt instruments that have been guaranteed (accepted) by a bank. While the commercial borrower may be perfectly reputable, the lender looks primarily to the bank for assurance of safety, and it's reasonable to view this category as another type of bank debt.

A word about the banks. In the money market, banks are by no means looked on as paragons of safety. The credit experts who analyze money market investments are keenly aware that a few banks have failed in recent years, and that many have come close to failing. There's a widespread feeling that many banks have taken too many risks in their lending policies. So buying bank debt is done very carefully, on a case-by-case basis, with the financial position of each bank studied in detail. The screening process appears to have worked, as money funds have not lost money by lending to banks, and we don't think that the money that the funds have out to banks is reason for any serious worry. Still, you may well be cautious of any money fund management that seems willing to take above-average risks in order to squeeze out a small extra bit of yield.

Commercial Paper

"Commercial paper" is the short-term debt of major corporations— corporations with sufficient reputation to be able to borrow in the money market on an "unsecured" basis, that is, without putting up any collateral. Obviously, there's a potential for risk here. But the companies that issue commercial paper are rated carefully and intensively by leading credit rating agencies (notably *Moody's* and *Standard & Poor's*), and the money funds typically buy only paper carrying very high ratings. So far there's been no trouble, nor should you expect any.

Curiously enough, it's probably easier to verify the financial condition of an industrial corporation than that of a bank. The balance sheet of a healthy corporation will show plentiful cash and/or assets that can easily be turned into cash, relative to the company's operating expenses and the money it owes. A good analyst or accountant can usually make a reasonable judgment as to whether the assets have the value they're supposed to have. In the case of a bank, this kind of judgment is more difficult. The bank's key asset is the money *owed to it* on loans it has made. Experience has shown that it can be terribly difficult for anyone outside the bank to judge the quality of those loans, and bank managements will rarely admit their mistakes. When you read the financial report of a money fund, you know *in detail* where the fund's money is invested. When you read a bank financial report, most of the details are missing. The moral of this digression is: don't worry about the commercial paper owned by your money fund—in the hands of experts who are intent on avoiding risks, it has proven to be a safe and efficient way of investing for the short term.

Repurchase Agreements

"Repurchase agreements" are a favorite way of lending and borrowing in the money market for the very short term, often overnight. The borrower—usually a bank or broker—puts up government securities as collateral, giving the lender a high degree of safety. The transaction is called a repurchase agreement or "repo" because it is structured so that the borrower technically *sells* the government securities (the collateral) to the lender and then *buys them back* (repurchases them) at the end of the transaction. All this is done at prearranged prices so that the lender will earn an agreed-upon rate of interest. Despite this technical form, the SEC looks on a repo as just a different type of loan, and we won't argue with them. Repos have come under a cloud in the past because of certain loopholes in the protection enjoyed by the lender. But the bankruptcy law was changed in mid-1984 to reduce the loopholes, and there's now less reason for concern.

In fact, given a good money fund management, there's probably nothing at all in the above list that you should worry about. But if you are worried anyway—see the next chapter.

Chapter Nine

The Government-Only Funds

Despite the impeccable safety record of regular money market funds, some people still worry about all that money out on loan to banks and nonbank corporations. Other people simply aren't comfortable unless their savings are guaranteed by the government, as they are in a bank or savings and loan association.

For people who feel this way, the money fund industry has come up with a good solution. In the early days of the industry, a few managers brought out "government" or "government-only" funds that are just what their name implies— money market funds investing only in U.S. government securities. In 1980, when soaring interest rates raised fears about many banks and savings and loans and even about the whole credit structure, the movement to form such funds began to accelerate, until by mid-1984 there were over 70 money funds, most of them relatively new, following some version of a "government-only" policy. (For information about some of these, see Table C at the back of this book.)

Even within this limited category, there are variations. Some of the funds invest only in securities issued directly by the U.S. Treasury—which means, in practice, primarily Treasury bills. A second group extends its range slightly to include securities of those rather few federal agencies that carry the "full faith and credit" (that is, the complete backing) of the U.S. government.

Perhaps you didn't know that there are several federal agencies that issue securities that do *not*, technically speaking, carry the full backing of the Treasury. Would Congress ever let one of these agencies default on its debt? It's a favorite argument among money market sophisticates. At any rate, there's a third group of "government-only" funds that do buy the securities of these agencies as well, raising the yield to their shareholders slightly in the process.

Though no one can be absolutely and completely certain, the authors are among those who don't think that a federal agency will ever be allowed to default, and as a result we don't think there's a significant degree of risk difference among these three groups of "government-only" funds. It's interesting that most of the funds in all three groups have made a regular practice of engaging in repurchase transactions, which until at least mid-1984 *did* carry a certain very small degree of risk (See Chapter 8). But the risk level in all of these funds seems to us to be as close to zero as one is likely to get.

What price do you pay if you go for the extra-extra safety of a government-only money fund? Interestingly enough, you don't lose as much yield as you might think. For example, in mid-June 1984, according to the weekly *Donoghue's Money Fund Report,* the average latest current yield on the most conservative "regular" money funds was almost exactly 10.0%.* Money funds with more varied portfolios, and presumably carrying an extra drop of risk, were averaging 10.1% or 10.2%. By comparison, the government money funds following a "Treasuries-only" policy were yielding a shade *under* 9.7%, and the government funds that also buy agency securities were yielding a shade *over* 9.7%. In sum, you would have gained only about 0.3% in yield by going from a government-only fund to a conservative "regular" fund, or only about 0.5% by going to one of the more aggressive funds.

Why the rather small differential? Is it because the regular funds really carry so little additional risk? That may be one reason, but another reason is the tremendous U.S. government budget deficit. Because of the deficit, the Treasury has had to borrow hundreds of billions of dollars in recent years to cover its expenses. As in any other supply-demand situation, the more the government has had to borrrow, the higher the relative interest rates it has had to pay. Since Treasury debt is still regarded as zero-risk debt against which all other types of debt are measured on the risk scale, the money market can't make the Treasury pay *more* than other borrowers pay. But because of the Treasury's heavy borrowings, the differential between the rates it pays and the rates that prime borrowers pay has narrowed.

What this means, in short, is that the rates you can earn by lending short-term to the U.S. government (through a government-only fund) have moved up close to the rates you can earn by lending short-term to banks and corporations (through a regular money fund). That being the case, we won't bother reminding you that the regular money funds have a perfect safety record, and that the risks are generally infinitesimal. If you want the extra assurance

---

*This and the following percentage figures show current yield without compounding, based on the funds' actual earnings over a seven-day period. The "effective annual yield" at each of these rates, adjusted to include the effect of daily compounding, would be noticeably higher. (See Chapter 12.)

of a government-only fund, it won't cost you much, and we won't try to argue you out of it. If the government fund helps you sleep better, 0.3% or even 0.5% is a small price to pay.

And we hasten to add that there may be more specific reasons for choosing a government-only fund. Let's say you are a rich individual or an institution with more than $100,000 to invest and you want absolute safety. You are mindful that a bank deposit is only insured up to $100,000. A government money fund solves your problem easily and simply. Your money is invested in U.S. government securities in any amount you wish. Of course, you could split your money among several banks so that each account is fully insured, or you could invest in Treasury securities directly. But in a money fund your money is professionally managed, you don't have to worry about which government securities are the best buy today and which might be the best buy tomorrow, and you enjoy all its other conveniences.

There's another reason for buying a government-only fund—maybe. It's a tax reason, and it needs a word of explanation. If you own U.S. government securities *directly*, the interest you receive is taxed by the IRS like any other interest, but it is *exempt* from *state and local* income taxes. Where state income tax rates are high, this has been an incentive for owning government securities, especially for investors in high tax brackets.

The government money funds argue that since they are only receiving interest on U.S. government securities and passing that interest through to their shareholders as dividends, their distributions also should be exempt from state and local income taxes. It's a nice point for lawyers. As of mid-1984, a California court had ruled in favor of the funds (and a tax exemption for shareholders), but the decision seemed likely to be appealed. In New York, the tax authorities were maintaining that the interest changes character when it is transformed into fund dividends, and therefore it's fully taxable by the state. This issue will not be fully resolved for quite a while.

If you are, or will be, a money fund investor, and if you live where the state and/or local income tax rates are high, if may be worth your while to check with one of the government money funds, or else with an accountant or attorney, for information on this particular tax wrinkle. In New York state, for example, where the income tax rates go as high as 14%, a government-only money fund might turn out to be one of the best deals in town, especially for a high-bracket taxpayer. Let's say you are a New Yorker choosing among money funds yielding the average mid-1984 rates shown on page 24. The regular money fund would yield a fully taxable 10.0%. The government-only fund would yield 9.7%, but, if the law changes, you would *not* pay the 14% state tax on this income. Since 14% × 9.7% = 1.3% (roughly), it would be like adding 1.3% to your net yield. But not quite: if you paid the 1.3% to the state, you probably would deduct this state tax on your federal income tax return, and the net cost of the state tax to you might be only 0.7% or 0.8%, depending on your federal tax bracket. However, you would still be well ahead of the game. Add in this saving of 0.7% or 0.8%, and your government-only money fund would give you as much income after taxes as a regular money fund earning 10.4% or 10.5%.

So if you live in New York, California, or some other high-tax state, keep this point in mind, and try to follow what happens as the issue moves through the courts. Your eventual savings might make you glad that you plowed through the above explanation.

Chapter Ten

The Tax-Exempt Money Market Funds

The interest on bonds and other debt instruments issued by state and local governments, and their agencies, is exempt from federal income tax.

All sorts of financial institutions and arrangements have been built around this fact. The market in "tax-exempt" or "municipal" securities—"municipals" for short—is a tremendous one. Individuals, especially those in higher tax brackets, are large buyers of municipals. So are such institutions as banks and insurance companies. The yields on tax-exempt securities are generally lower than those on comparable taxable debt securities, but for some the tax advantage more than makes up for the differential.

In the late 1970s, a federal law was passed allowing mutual funds specializing in tax-exempt debt securities to pass through the tax advantage to their shareholders. Suddenly a whole new segment of the mutual-fund industry began to grow. The first tax-exempt funds principally held long-term bonds. But by 1981 a new group of *short-term* tax-exempt funds—that is, *tax-free money market funds*—was growing rapidly. In a very short time, these tax-free funds have become an established part of the money market fund industry. (For information about some of these, see Table D at the back of this book.)

In their structure and the way they work, the tax-free money funds are not noticeably different from the regular money funds. Since the funds are intended to attract primarily high-tax-bracket investors who can benefit from the tax advantage, the minimums are often higher than in the average regular funds. Apart from that—and the very different type of security in the portfolio—you won't notice much difference.

The decision as to whether these funds can benefit you is generally a matter of your tax bracket and a simple calculation. For example, let's consider the relative yields of taxable money funds and tax-free money funds in 1983. For the full calendar year, if you had owned the average of the 25 top-performing *"regular"* money funds, your effective yield for the year, including compounding, would have been just about 9.0%. Taking the top 25 *tax-free* money funds, it would have been about 5.0%.

What would the 5.0% be worth to you in taxable terms? Or, to use a more professional phrase, what would be your "taxable equivalent yield"? The computation really isn't hard. Let's assume that you are in a 38% federal income tax bracket. You calculate as follows:

$$\text{Taxable Equivalent Yield} = \frac{5.0\%}{100\% - 38\%} = 8.1\%$$

Obviously, in this case you would be better off with a regular money fund paying 9.0%. On the other hand, if you earned enough to be in the 49% federal tax bracket, the taxable equivalent yield would be 9.8%, and you would clearly be better off with the tax-free fund. (For convenience, we have included a table showing you the taxable equivalent yields of various tax-free yields for a few selected tax brackets. See Table H at the back of this book.)

The average tax-free money fund holds a rather bewildering array of short-term securities issued by states and localities in its portfolio. Many of these are rated for quality by the rating agencies, particularly *Moody's*. You should read the fund's prospectus and, unless you want to take some risk in pursuit of yield, make sure that the fund limits its investments to securities carrying the highest quality ratings.

While the dividends paid by a tax-free fund are exempt from *federal* income tax, the situation is not so clear when it comes to *state* income taxes. In most states, interest on the obligations issued by that state and its localities is exempt from that state's own income tax, but there are exceptions. Most states make you pay income tax on the interest you receive from out-of-state municipals, but a few don't. There's very little uniformity, and you have to check the rules that apply in your own state.

Double and Triple Tax-Free Funds

To avoid the state tax problem, there are now a few tax-free money funds that hold obligations of only a single state and its localities, so that the income is exempt from that state's income tax. As of mid-1984, such "double tax-free" funds had been established specifically to serve residents of California, Massachusetts, and New York. In New York, such funds are known as *triple* tax-free, since the income is exempt from New York City income tax as well. (See Table G at the back of this book.)

The double tax-free funds make good sense, and more will probably be formed in states where the local income tax rates are high. However, since these funds are limited to purchasing the obligations of one state, they may have trouble moving in and out of investments as flexibly as they would like. If you are considering such a fund, do enough comparisons with ordinary "single" tax-free funds to make sure that you are not sacrificing yield for the tax advantage, and that the managers are not reaching unreasonably for securities of longer maturity or lower quality in order to fill out the portfolio.

One more point. There are, of course, *long-term* tax-free funds —generally referred to as municipal bond funds. In fact, there are long-term and intermediate-term municipal funds, and one or two shorter-term funds that don't have all the features of a true money market fund. So if you are shopping for a tax-free money fund, check carefully to be certain that it *is* a money fund, and that it has all the conveniences you want and should expect.

Chapter Eleven

MMMF vs. MMDA

By now you know enough to figure out the rather cryptic chapter heading above. How do you choose between a money market mutual fund and a money market deposit account (market rate account) at a bank?

In Chapter 4 we sketched some of the history of competition between banks and money market funds, and we pointed out that the bank market rate accounts, first introduced in December 1982, have many of the same attractions as money funds. In fact, it's impossible to make any broad statement that one is better than the other. The answer depends very much on your own personal needs, and also on what the banks in your particular area are offering.

Return on Investment

Where will you get a better return on your money? That isn't the only factor to consider, and it may not even be the most critical for you, but it certainly is important. It's hard to make forecasts. As we said earlier, the money funds pay out whatever they can earn, while banks set rates on their money market accounts arbitrarily, usually on a weekly basis, based on whatever they think the competition requires.

As the following chart shows, in December 1982, banks started out by offering much higher rates than funds, and money came flooding into the new bank accounts as a result. But by late 1983 the bloom was off the rose, and the average money fund was paying more than the average bank market rate account, with the difference widening in early 1984.

For your own purposes, the key is in the word "average." It is very easy to find out what the funds are paying by following the weekly listings in your local newspaper (see Chapter 12). To find out what your local banks are paying, walk in and ask. Some banks specifically fix their rates at slightly above the latest published fund average—say by ¼ of 1% (0.25%). That arrangement obviously protects you reasonably well as far as yield is concerned, even recognizing that there are some funds which consistently pay more than the fund average.

Consider also the minimums that apply to the accounts. Many funds let you begin with as little as $1,000 or $500 (or even less—

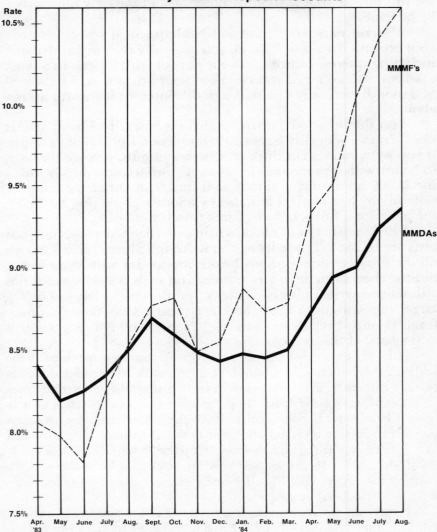

Average Rates, Money Market Mutual Funds, Bank Money Market Deposit Accounts

Rate

10.5%

MMMF's

10.0%

9.5%

MMDAs

9.0%

8.5%

8.0%

7.5%

Apr. May June July Aug. Sept. Oct. Nov. Dec. Jan. Feb. Mar. Apr. May June July Aug.
'83   '84

Source: Investment Company Institute (adapted)
Rates shown are current yields without compounding.
Annual effective yields would be higher as a result of compounding.

see Table A at the back of this book), and whatever balance you have in the fund earns the full rate. In contrast, you need $2,500 to start a bank market rate account (except for certain special retirement plan accounts), and for any period when your balance dips below $2,500 you earn only the 5¼% passbook rate rather than the full rate. If your account is not large, a fund may obviously be preferable.

A small point to consider is what happens if you close out your account. In a money fund, you generally receive your balance including interest earned up to the date of withdrawal. In a bank market rate account, if you close out your account before the end of a month, you may lose that month's interest. It's worth asking about.

You should also compare hidden expenses. The bank market rate accounts generally have strict transaction limits. For example, if you write more than three checks in a month, you are likely to be hit with a processing fee. And if your account dips below the $2,500 minimum, you may well find that you are penalized not only by loss of yield but also by another processing fee. Ask the bank for a full schedule of fees before you begin.

The comparison of check-writing privileges depends on your own needs. Banks generally let you write only three checks a month on their market rate accounts before you are hit with extra fees, but the checks can be in any amount you wish. Most money funds will let you write unlimited checks, but the checks have to be large. The minimum fund check is typically $500, though some funds permit checks for as little as $250 or even $100. (See Table B at the back of this book.)

A factor that most people will consider more important is the walk-in convenience of a bank. You can walk in to make deposits or take out cash. You can get cash from automatic teller machines (ATMs), a service the funds hope to offer but where banks clearly have a headstart. If you want to have these conveniences attached to your money market account, the banks obviously have an edge. We hasten to add that many people prefer to handle all these "walk-in" needs through their regular bank checking account, using a money market fund for their excess cash reserves and for writing occasional large checks.

Note that we are comparing money market funds only with bank market rate accounts, and not with other services offered by banks. Of course, banks offer regular checking accounts and other services that the funds don't offer. If you want to have all your cash management services under the same roof, you are obviously likely to prefer a bank market rate account. And in Chapter 7 we mentioned situations in which you should consider putting part of your money in bank certificates of deposit to raise your yield, rather than limiting yourself to either a money fund or a bank market rate account.

However, if your long-run planning includes the goal of investment diversity and flexibility (and it should—see Chapter 17), then the money market funds have one very clear advantage over the banks. As we pointed out in Chapter 6, when you choose a money fund that is part of a larger fund group, you have the advantage of easy *switching* among the funds in the group. We won't repeat all the points we made earlier, but we'll simply note that many money fund investors wouldn't consider doing without the convenience and flexibility that this privilege provides.

One more point—and it's an important one. You'll note that we haven't yet said a word in this chapter about *safety*—the area where some people feel that the difference between a bank and a money market fund is most critical.

There's no doubt that in your cash management, complete safety is absolutely essential. It's not an area in which to take risks. Banks and savings and loans have their accounts insured up to $100,000 each by the FDIC or FSLIC. Money market funds aren't insured.

Nevertheless, we find it hard to view this difference as critically important. The perfect safety record of the money funds, after more than ten years of experience, is deeply impressive. The general safety record of money market investments is excellent. If a money fund limits its investments to obligations of the U.S. government, the highest-rated banks, and the highest-rated corporations, it's hard to believe that safety is a matter of great concern. And if you still want extra assurance, you have the option of a government-only fund (see Chapter 9), where you can forget about risk completely—and where you can enjoy the "full faith and credit" of the U.S. government on amounts above $100,000, which is something no single bank can do for you.

What if you choose a money fund that seems to take slightly higher risks? If your overriding concern is safety, you obviously won't make such a choice. But if you think that an extra ¼% of yield (or thereabouts) is worth a tiny extra bit of risk, you can choose a money fund that buys the debt obligations of a wider range of banks and corporations—including some that may not carry the highest ratings, but that the fund management regards as safe. This is a question of individual preference, and it doesn't really relate to the broader question of the safety of money funds as compared with banks.

One of the reasons we don't emphasize the safety problem is that if a money fund ever were to suffer one or two portfolio losses, it wouldn't be catastrophic. Take as an example a large money fund, which might diversify its holdings into 100 different short-term investments, with each one accounting on average for only 1% of the total portfolio. A complete default on one of these items would, in effect, cut 1% from your yield for the year—from 7% to 6%, or from 10% to 9%, as the case may be. Even if the fund had 5% of its assets with one borrower (the maximum percentage allowed by law), a complete default would only mean a 5% loss of yield for that year—a serious disappointment, but not a complete disaster. And we repeat that the likelihood of any such loss seems very remote indeed.

There's another safety question that is often raised and is worth mentioning. What happens if the *manager* of a money fund runs into financial difficulties? For example, if the money fund is managed by a brokerage firm, what happens if the brokerage firm goes bankrupt?

We aren't suggesting that any such event is likely. But if it did happen, it's important to note that under the structure required by the law and monitored by the SEC, the fund is carefully separated and insulated from the management firm. The fund is a completely separate corporation (or in some cases a trust), and its assets can't be touched except for the benefit of the shareholders. The assets are held under the supervision of a custodian (in all or virtually all cases, a bank), and both the fund and the bank must be insured against theft or loss. This regulatory structure has worked perfectly well over the years, and you don't need to worry about it. Still, if you should hear that the manager of your fund is in trouble, it would make sense to switch to another fund.

So much for the safety question. After all the pluses and minuses, what's left on a practical basis? Our own conclusion is that in choosing between a money market fund and a bank market rate account, there are several important differences to consider, as spelled out above, but that the safety difference is not really very significant. Still, if you want the absolute maximum in safety, you have a choice between an insured bank account and a government-only money fund, and you should be able to make a choice without having to give up any of the other advantages you require.

Chapter Twelve

Selecting a Money Market Fund: Comparing Yields

Throughout this book we have pointed out many items to compare in picking the right money fund for you. In this chapter and the next we'll add some details and touch on a few points that haven't yet been considered.

First, the question of "yield." Yield is the return you receive on an investment, usually expressed as a percentage. In a money market fund, it is the dividends you receive. How do you know what rates the various funds are paying currently, or what rates they have yielded in past periods? For the current rates, go to your newspaper. You will *not* find the money funds in the daily listings of mutual fund prices that appear in many newspapers. Those listings are primarily to show daily price changes, and the prices of money fund shares stay constant at $1.00 per share (see Chapter 15). But every Friday, in the *Wall Street Journal* and in other newspapers with sizable business and financial sections, you will find a table showing the current yields of money funds with assets over $100 million. The table, provided by *Donoghue's Money Fund Report,* shows each fund's latest reported total assets (in millions of dollars), the average maturity of its portfolio (in days), the latest seven-day average yield (in percentages), and the latest thirty-day average yield (in percentages).

The seven-day yield is a standard industry comparison figure, computed according to guidelines set by the SEC. It shows the rate earned by shareholders during the very latest seven-day period, *without* any adjustment for compounding. The thirty-day yield is figured similarly, but using the longer base period. If interest rates are rising, the latest seven-day yields for most funds will be above the thirty-day figures, and vice versa. Note that a fund's yield doesn't change instantaneously in response to fluctuations in market interest rates, but with a slight lag, as the investments in the fund's portfolio mature and are replaced with new investments at the current rate.

The shorter the average maturity of the portfolio, as shown in the Donoghue table, the more quickly the fund's yield should respond to changes in the market. The average maturity also may tell you something about a fund's average risk level. The general rule in the money market is that the shorter the maturity, the lower the risk and the less the possibility of fluctuations in value. If a fund shows a higher-than-average yield but also a higher-than-average maturity, it may possibly be taking a very slight risk in favor of higher yield; you can't be sure from the table, but you should take a careful look at the fund's prospectus. (See Chapter 15.)

The Donoghue table that we have been discussing covers only a limited list of funds, and it does *not* include any of the tax-free funds. In the *Wall Street Journal,* every Monday, hidden among the stock market tables, you can find a small table titled "Money Market Funds" that gives less information per fund but lists a somewhat larger number of funds, including several tax-free funds. This list, compiled by the National Association of Securities Dealers, gives only the name of the fund, the average maturity, and the latest seven-day yield. Yields are on the same noncompounded basis as in the Donoghue table.

These noncompounded, or "simple," yields are sometimes referred to as the "current yield." Since they ignore the effect of daily compounding, they don't really tell you what you can earn in a fund over the course of a year. For that purpose, the funds also regularly calculate what is termed the "effective yield," or "effective annual yield." This calculation takes the latest seven-day yield figure and projects what would actually be earned if that rate were maintained for a full year, taking daily compounding into account. The difference can be significant, and is particularly important if you are comparing money fund rates with bank rates that are expressed on an "effective annual yield" basis.

The latest effective annual yield can usually be obtained by a telephone call to the fund. Most funds have toll-free "800" numbers, and many use a special number for a recording giving latest yield information. The fund's quarterly or semi-annual reports to shareholders also usually provide yield information on both a simple and compounded basis. To help you translate the seven-day base figures into effective annual yields on your own, Table J (at the back of this book) will be helpful.

If you want to check longer-term statistics, there are several sources available, some of which you may find in your local library. As you may have gathered in reading this book, the Donoghue Organization is the leading compiler and provider of money market fund statistics. Donoghue's weekly *Money Fund*

Report, which gives the current information provided to the newspapers and much more, is an expensive service intended mainly for professionals. But Donoghue's *Mutual Funds Almanac* is an annual handbook available for $23. It includes listings of money market funds (and other types of funds), with some descriptive information and figures on annual performance over the last ten years. (The Donoghue Organization, Inc., Box 540, Holliston, MA 01746—phone 617-429-5930.)

Another annual handbook providing similar tables and somewhat more detailed information about the individual funds is the *Handbook for No-Load Fund Investors.* This excellent book covers all categories of no-load funds and is available for $29. (The No-Load Fund Investor, Inc., P.O. Box 283, Hastings-on-Hudson, NY 10706—phone 914-478-2381.)

In these books (and usually in other sources where annual performance figures are given), the annual yield figures are given on a compounded or "effective annual yield" basis. They are intended to show how money would have grown if left in the fund for a full year. If, for example, a fund reported its current yield at 10% steadily throughout the year, its effective annual yield would have been just about 10.5%, and $1,000 invested at the beginning of the year would have ended the year as $1,105 (a gain of $105).

Where a single percentage figure is given to summarize performance over two years or more, the same compounding approach is applied. If a fund showed a 10.5% effective annual yield for five years in a row, $1,000 invested at the beginning of the period would have grown over the five years to $1,647, and the five-year gain would be stated as 64.7% (*not* 52.5%, which is the incorrect answer you would get if you simply multiplied 10.5% by five). Approaching it from the other direction, if you are given a performance figure for five or ten years, you can't calculate the average annual return by dividing by five or ten; you need compound interest tables, or a sophisticated calculator. Be careful when dealing with performance figures covering more than a single year.

Chapter Thirteen

Selecting a Money Market Fund: Other Comparisons

In picking a money market fund that is right for you, current yields and past performance records are obviously important considerations, but they are not the only items to consider.

We have discussed most other important characteristics of a fund in earlier chapters. You want to pick a fund that is large enough, or affiliated with a large enough fund group, so that you will know it has the capacity to give you the services you expect. If you agree with us as to the importance of the switching privilege, you will want to pick a fund that is part of a high-quality group, and your choice of a money fund may very likely be dictated by your choice of common stock or bond funds in which you have decided to invest. Table E at the back of this book lists a few such funds. (For more on this subject, see the NO-NONSENSE FINANCIAL GUIDE TO MUTUAL FUNDS.)

If switching isn't your primary concern, you may be influenced by the fund's minimum deposit requirements (see Table A at the back of this book), or by the flexibility it gives you in check-writing privileges (see Table B). Another factor worth considering is the location of the fund and of its custodian bank. If either one is located close to you in your own city, you may be able to get quick credit for deposits without the delay caused by the mails. If that kind of convenience isn't possible, you may still prefer to pick a fund located where you have some reason to hope that the mail service may be prompt.

Most of the answers to the above questions are answered by the handbooks mentioned in the previous chapter. But these only take you part way. After you have identified a few funds that seem to meet your requirements, phone each fund (in most cases the "800" numbers make it simple and free) and ask for its prospectus. Typically the fund will send you the prospectus (a legal document that is the basic description of the fund and its policies) and its latest annual and interim reports to shareholders, as well as some miscellaneous sales literature.

A prospectus can be frustrating. Over the years, mutual fund prospectuses have become weighted down with large quantities of legal verbiage that don't really help you understand the fund and its policies. But improvement is under way. Beginning in late 1984, the SEC has ordered the funds to provide a shorter, simplified prospectus, with additional detailed information available from the fund on request. This should help. Read the short form, and phone the fund office for the "Statement of Additional Information" if you still have questions that haven't been answered.

The most important sections to read in the prospectus are those describing investment policies and fund objectives. See whether the fund stresses maximum safety or maximum yield. Look at the list of investments in either the prospectus or the financial reports. Many of the items on the list will probably be unfamiliar to you, but you may be able to get a sense of whether the fund is reaching far afield in search of higher yield, or whether it is content to limit its investments to the most reputable banks and corporations. The prospectus will also tell you something about the fund's management, and about any affiliations it may have with a fund group, a brokerage firm, or other organizations.

In addition, use the prospectus to check the fund's rules and procedures with respect to minimums, check-writing privileges, telephone redemptions, signature guarantees, and other technical arrangements. Whatever information you may have seen in the reference books or in newspaper or magazine surveys, remember that it's what the prospectus says that counts. While it may be hard reading, there's merit to the simple warning that all mutual funds are required to put in their advertisements: "Read it carefully before you invest or send money."

Chapter Fourteen

Deposits and Withdrawals

We chose the title of this chapter deliberately because it isn't true. When you put money in a money market fund, or take money out, you are *not*, technically speaking, making deposits and withdrawals as you would in a bank. Since you are a shareholder (owner) of the fund, you are actually buying shares or redeeming (selling) them. Keeping this in mind may help you understand certain of the procedures. But we hasten to add that the purchases and redemptions of shares are easy to think of as deposits and withdrawals, and if you want to refer to them that way, it's all right with us. In fact, we may use that wording ourselves.

To open an account in a money fund, you usually use the order form that arrives with the prospectus. The order form should tell you how to make your check payable and where to mail it. The order form also gives you the opportunity to request special services such as check-writing, telephone redemptions, etc., and it asks whether you want your dividends mailed to you or reinvested.

If you are accustomed to other types of mutual funds where you can sometimes order shares by telephone and be billed for the purchase, don't expect that service from a money fund. A money fund can't invest your money for you and begin paying you dividends until it actually has your money in hand. So purchases by telephone aren't permitted.

If you are purchasing by check, the fund won't begin crediting you with dividends until your check has cleared and has been converted into "federal funds," which means that the fund's bank has been credited with the money at its Federal Reserve bank. There are variations in how quickly this takes place, but a typical policy is for the fund to credit you with shares two business days after it receives your check, and to begin crediting you with dividends one day later.

If you want to have your money credited more immediately, you can have your bank *wire* money to the fund's bank. The procedures to be followed are listed in the prospectus, and you should phone the fund office for detailed instructions. Nothing can be more exasperating than to wire money to a fund and to have it sit inactive at the fund's bank for lack of proper identification. It is particularly important to follow instructions carefully when wiring money to open a new account, since you don't yet have a fund account number for identification.

Another small point about opening an account. Remember that a money market fund isn't a bank. If you open a joint account, it doesn't operate in the same "either/or" way as a bank joint account, where either owner can deposit or withdraw freely. Money market funds, like other mutual funds, follow the procedures that are customary in the securities industry, where no significant action can be taken on a joint account without the signatures of all the owners. However, this isn't a problem on deposits, where no signature is called for; and if you are opening a joint account and ordering checks, most order forms will let you specify, if you wish, that a single signature be accepted on checks. (Don't forget to include *both* signatures on the order form.)

As for taking money out of the fund, we have covered redemption methods quite fully in Chapter 6. You can redeem by check, by telephone, by wire, or by letter. To use any of the first three methods, you will probably need to request the privilege on the order form. If you want to close out your account completely you must use some method other than a check, since you are credited with dividends daily, and you won't know the exact balance in the account at the time when you write the check. It's wise to read the prospectus carefully regarding the fund's procedures for various types of redemptions; don't risk the frustration of not being able to get at your money when you want it.

As we've indicated elsewhere, the most significant type of redemption you make from your money fund may be when you switch money to some other type of mutual fund as part of your investment management planning. If you have picked a money fund that is part of a fund group, read the prospectus to find out the switching procedures and whether any fees are involved. Indicate on your order form that you want the privilege of switching funds by telephone, or file a special authorization form if that is required. If you think that you might be making frequent switches between funds, see if the order form or the prospectus puts any limit on how often you can switch; if necessary, call the fund office for information. It's better to take a little extra trouble at the beginning than to have unpleasant surprises later.

Chapter Fifteen

Why Net Asset Value Equals $1.00

There's a technical point about money market funds that we have not mentioned up to now, but that needs to be dealt with briefly.

As we said in the previous chapter, when you "deposit" money in a money fund, you are actually buying shares. You give the fund a check for $1,000, for example, and you are credited with 1,000 shares. In other types of mutual funds, the price per share changes every day. How do you know, in a money fund, that the shares will still be worth $1.00 each when you are ready to redeem? Obviously, if the shares were to drop in value to $0.99 each, your $1,000 would have been transformed to $990, and the money fund would no longer qualify as safe.

The money funds follow careful policies and procedures to make sure that their shares will remain valued at $1.00. That's what the safety of the funds is all about. Some of these procedures are described in each fund's prospectus, but the explanations can be complicated. And you'll note that under SEC rules each prospectus is required to say, in effect, that the fund *intends* to keep its share value at $1.00, but that this can't be guaranteed.

To see how a money fund maintains that $1.00 value, let's look at mutual funds in general. The value of a mutual fund's shares is calculated in a very simple way. Every day the fund adds up the market values of all the individual securities (stocks, bonds, etc.) it owns. It also adds in the value of its other assets— its cash and any amounts it is owed. From the total it subtracts any liabilities—amounts that it owes to others for various fees and other expenses. The result is the "total net assets" of the fund. This figure is then divided by the "shares outstanding" (the total number of shares held by shareholders) to arrive at the "net asset value per share," which is each share's proportionate interest in the fund's total net assets.

In a "common stock" type of mutual fund, the market value of the common stocks owned by the fund fluctuates from day to day, and the net asset value per share (that is, the price per share) of the fund fluctuates as well. In fact, one of the objectives of the shareholders is to see the price of their shares go up, which will happen if the fund managers invest successfully in common stocks that rise in market value.

Investors in money market funds aren't looking for that kind of profit. They want complete safety and stability. So, as you already know, the fund does *not* invest in common stocks or long-term bonds, but only in short-term debt instruments of the highest quality.

What makes it necessary for the fund to follow very careful procedures is that even these high-quality money market investments can, in fact, vary ever so slightly in market value from day to day. For example, assume that on April 1 a money fund buys a $1 million bank CD due in 30 days and paying 8%, and that on April 2 interest rates generally rise and banks are now issuing comparable CDs at 8½%. With 8½% CDs available, no one will pay full price for an 8% CD, and the market value of the 8% CD will fall ever so slightly below $1 million—even though there's no doubt at all that the issuing bank will pay off the $1 million in another 29 days.

In a case like this, the sooner the CD is due ("matures"), the smaller the market price variation. This is the reason most money funds keep the portfolio "average maturity" well below 60 days. In addition, if the funds keep their average maturity very short, the SEC permits them to use certain accounting methods that smooth out the day-to-day price variations. You will see these methods described in the prospectus as "amortized cost," "penny rounding," or "constant net asset value." If you don't want to read the prospectus descriptions of how they work, it probably doesn't matter; you simply need to know that all three methods are designed to help the fund maintain the $1.00 per share price. On the other hand, you should probably be just a shade wary of the relatively few funds that use the "variable net asset value" method—they are telling you that there is a slightly greater possibility that their price per share could change.

In Chapter 11 we discussed the safety of the money market funds, and gave our reasons for believing that there is exceptionally little to worry about. Now that you know why the price of a money fund's shares could theoretically vary away from $1.00, we again feel perfectly comfortable in saying that if you buy a conservative money fund that keeps its average maturity short and limits itself to high-rated investments, there's no need to worry.

What if you buy a less conservative money fund that deliberately takes a shade more risk in order to squeeze out the very highest yield? This type of fund may earn ¼% or ½% more for you than the average fund. If, unexpectedly, the value of the fund's shares were to fall to $0.99 each, you would have lost 1% of your money. The risk is still very small, and if the extra yield seems worth it to you—go ahead.

Chapter Sixteen

Record-keeping and Taxes

This chapter will be short. In a money market fund, record-keeping and tax matters are about as simple as they can be.

Your monthly or quarterly statements from the fund will give you a clear record of all transactions. It's a good idea to keep each year's statements for at least three years after that year's income tax return is filed, just in case you are subject to a tax audit.

If you use the check-writing privilege, any cancelled checks that are evidence for income tax deductions also should be kept for three years after the tax return is filed. (We really aren't happy with those funds that don't return your cancelled checks.)

Every January, if your dividends for the preceding year have exceeded $10, the fund should send you a copy of Form 1099, the information form on which the fund reports your dividends to the IRS (Internal Revenue Service). You'll note that your dividends are described as "nonqualifying"—that is, they do *not* qualify for the "dividend exclusion" that lets taxpayers exclude up to $100 of dividends from taxable income (up to $200 on a joint return). The reason is that a mutual fund's dividends are eligible (qualifying) to the extent that the fund is passing through *dividend* income to its shareholders, and not eligible (nonqualifying) to the extent that the fund is passing through *interest* (or miscellaneous income). Since money market fund dividends derive completely from interest, they are completely nonqualifying.

That's all about record-keeping and taxes. Now, with a sigh of relief, we can turn away from technical matters, and return to a subject that is more vital to your future—money market funds as an *investment*.

Chapter Seventeen

Beyond the Money Market Funds

Early in this book, we talked about *cash management* and *investment management*.

Much of this book has shown how money market funds meet your needs for *cash management*—management of money that you are using currently or might need in the near future. They do this by giving you safety, liquidity, convenience and relatively high yield.

Are these features sufficient to meet your needs for *investment management* as well? Many people now keep part or all of their long-run investment dollars in money market funds. In certain years this has been remarkably profitable. In both 1980 and 1982, most money funds earned well over 12% for their shareholders, and in 1981, when interest rates averaged their highest, many funds actually earned *over 17%*.

In a money fund, you know that your money will consistently earn very close to the market rate of interest. What does this mean for you over the long run? Based on past experience, it means that *your money will probably grow enough to keep up with the rate of inflation and perhaps a little more*. Because of inflation, the real value (or purchasing power) of each dollar you put in a money fund will suffer some shrinkage each year; but the dividends you receive, if reinvested, should offset the shrinkage and perhaps more than offset it.

A money fund won't give you dramatic profits, but it should keep the real value of your savings from eroding. In an inflationary era, that isn't bad. By comparison, in the mid-1970s, before the banks were deregulated and the money funds became popular, people who kept their money in bank passbook accounts saw the real value of their money erode dangerously.

But you should never take your investments for granted. The exceptionally high yields of the money funds in 1980–82 were an unusual phenomenon that may not often be repeated. Over the long run, money market investments have not made money grow to the same degree as certain other types of investments. For example, over a very long period common stock investments have not only kept up with inflation but, on the average, have earned a return for their holders *6% above the rate of inflation*.

Of course, common stock investments involve risks and uncertainties that don't exist in a money fund. But in planning your long-run investments, one of the questions you should regularly consider is whether you are willing to take some extra degree of risk in the hope of making your money grow at a substantially better rate. There's no simple answer to this question; the answer depends on your own preferences and your financial needs.

If you want to avoid the uncertainties of common stocks and other "growth" investments, and prefer to stay with stable investments that have highly predictable interest earnings, you still might prefer to raise your yield by putting part of your money in bank certificates that run for perhaps two or three years. In periods when interest rates are rising, this may hold down your earnings; but if you do it consistently over a long period, you should earn more on the money than if it were in a money market fund or bank market rate account. As for the "lock-in" feature, remember that this is money you weren't going to use in the near future anyway.

Or you might consider buying U.S. Treasury notes—Treasury obligations due to mature in one to seven years, and easily available through a bank or broker. At certain times, these notes have yielded substantially more than available through the money funds. For reasons touched on in Chapter 15, the market prices of these notes may vary moderately as interest rates fluctuate, but, needless to say, you don't have to worry about whether the notes will be paid off at maturity.

Our intention is not to recommend any particular investment choices to you, but to stress the importance of thoughtful investment planning. Review your own needs regularly and carefully. Don't necessarily stay with an investment for the future simply because it has done well for you in the past.

Money market funds are one of the great innovations on the U.S. financial scene. You should consider their advantages and use them in the way that best fits your own needs. If you do, they can make a major contribution to your financial future.

HAPPY INVESTING!

Glossary

Adviser—See investment adviser.

Automatic Reinvestment—A plan by which income dividends and/or capital gains distributions are automatically applied to buy additional shares of a mutual fund.

Bankers' Acceptances—See Chapter 8.

Bond—A long-term debt security issued by a government or corporation promising repayment of a given amount by a given date, plus interest.

Bond Fund—A mutual fund investing primarily in bonds.

Brokerage Firm—A term including several types of firms in the securities business that usually do business with the public.

Capital—Wealth invested or available for investment.

Certificates of Deposit (CDs)—Negotiable interest-bearing certificates by which a bank promises to repay money deposited with it for a specific time period at a specified interest rate.

Collateral—Property that a borrower gives or assigns to a lender as security for a loan. If the borrower defaults (fails to repay), the lender takes the collateral.

Commercial Paper—See Chapter 8.

Common Stock—A security representing a share of ownership in a corporation.

Common Stock Fund—A mutual fund investing primarily in common stocks.

Custodian—The organization (usually a bank) that holds in safekeeping the securities and other assets of a mutual fund.

Diversification—The practice of spreading investments over several different securities to reduce risk.

Dividend—A share of earnings paid to a shareholder by a mutual fund or other corporation.

Dividend Reinvestment—See Automatic Reinvestment.

Investment Adviser—The organization that a mutual fund pays for investment advice and, usually, general business management. The adviser is usually also the sponsor and promoter of the fund.

Investment Advisory Fee—The fee paid by a mutual fund (or other investor) to an adviser.

Investment Company—A company in which many investors pool their money for investment. Mutual funds are the most popular type.

Liquid Asset Fund—A money market fund.

Liquid Investment—An investment that can be converted easily into cash, without penalty.

Load—The sales charge or commission charged on purchase of some mutual funds.

Management Fee—See Investment Advisory Fee.

Maturity—The maturity date is the date when a debt obligation becomes due for repayment. The "average maturity" of a portfolio at any given date is the average time to maturity of all the securities in the portfolio.

Money Fund—A money market fund.

Money Market Fund—A mutual fund that aims at maximum safety, liquidity, and a constant price for its shares. Its assets are invested to earn current market interest rates on the safest, short-term, highly liquid investments.

Municipal Bond—A bond issued by a state or local government. The interest is exempt from federal income tax.

Mutual Fund—An open-end investment company that pools the investments of many investors to provide them with professional management, diversification and other advantages.

Net Asset Value—See Chapter 15.

No-Load Fund—A mutual fund that sells its shares at net asset value, without any commission.

Open-End Investment Company—A mutual fund. Technically called "open-end" because the fund stands ready to sell new shares to investors or to buy back shares submitted for redemption.

Portfolio—The total list of securities owned by a mutual fund or by any investor.

Portfolio Manager—An individual who makes decisions regarding buying, selling, or holding securities for an investment organization.

Principal—The capital or main body of an investment, as distinguished from the income earned on it.

Prospectus—The official document describing a mutual fund and offering its shares for sale.

Redemption—The procedure by which a mutual fund buys back shares from shareholders on demand.

Repurchase Agreement ("Repo")—See Chapter 8.

SEC—The U.S. Securities and Exchange Commission: The federal agency charged with regulating securities markets and the investment industry.

Security—General term meaning stocks, bonds and other investment instruments.

Stock—A security representing an ownership interest in a corporation.

Yield—The return on an investment. In securities, the dividends or interest received, usually expressed as a percentage of the value of the investment.

TABLE A

Selected Money Market Funds With Starting Minimums of $500 or Less and More Than $100 Million in Assets

Name	Minimum Initial Investment/ Subsequent Investment	Portfolio	Check-writing Minimum	Toll-free Telephone Number
Centennial Money Market Trust	$500/none	diversified	no checks	800-525-9310
Daily Cash Accumulation Fund	$500/$100	diversified	$250	800-525-9310
Franklin Federal Money Fund	$500/$100	government	$100	800-227-6781
Franklin Money Fund	$500/$100	diversified	$100	800-227-6781

TABLE B

SELECTED MONEY MARKET FUNDS WITH CHECK-WRITING MINIMUMS OF $100 OR LESS AND MORE THAN $100 MILLION IN ASSETS

Name	Check-writing Minimum	Portfolio	Minimum Initial Investment/ Subsequent Investment	Toll-free Telephone Number
Boston Company Cash Management Fund	$100	diversified	$1000/none	800-343-6324
Calvert Tax-free Reserves—Money Market Portfolio	no minimum	municipals	$2000/$250	800-368-2748
Capital Preservation Fund	$100	government	$1000/$100	800-4-SAFETY
Capital Preservation Fund II	$100	government	$5000/$100	800-4-SAFETY
Carnegie Government Securities Trust—Money Market Series	$100	government	$1000/$250	800-321-2322
Composite Cash Management Company	no minimum	diversified	$1000/$500	800-541-0830
Fidelity Daily Income Trust	no minimum	diversified	$10,000/$500	800-225-6190
Fidelity U.S. Government Reserves	no minimum	government	$1000/$250	800-225-6190
Franklin Federal Money Fund	$100	government	$500/$100	800-227-6781
Franklin Money Fund	$100	diversified	$500/$100	800-227-6781
Liquid Capital Income Trust	$100	diversified	$1000/$250	800-321-2322
SteinRoe Tax-exempt Money Fund, Inc.	$100	municipals	$2500/$100	800-621-0320

TABLE C

SELECTED MONEY MARKET FUNDS INVESTING IN U.S. GOVERNMENT SECURITIES ONLY AND WITH MORE THAN $100 MILLION IN ASSETS

Name	Minimum Initial Investment/ Subsequent Investment	Check-writing Minimum	Toll-free Telephone Number
Alliance Government Reserves, Inc.	$1000/100	$500	800-221-9513
Capital Preservation Fund	$1000/100	$100	800-4-SAFETY
Capital Preservation Fund II	$5000/100	$100	800-4-SAFETY
Cardinal Government Securities Trust	$1000/100	$500	800-848-7734
Carnegie Government Securities Trust	$1000/250	$100	800-321-2322
Cash Equivalent Fund, Inc.— Government Securities Portfolio	$1000/100	$500	800-621-1048
DBL Cash Fund, Inc.—Government Securities Portfolio	$1000/100	$500	800-272-2700
Dean Witter/Sears U.S. Government Money Market Trust	$1000/50	$500	800-221-2685
Dreyfus Money Market Instruments Inc.—Government Securities Series	$2500/100	$500	800-645-6561
Fidelity U.S. Government Reserves	$1000/250	no minimum	800-225-6190
First Variable Rate Fund for Government Income, Inc.	$2000/250	no minimum	800-368-2748

TABLE C (*Continued*)

Name	Minimum Initial Investment/ Subsequent Investment	Check-writing Minimum	Toll-free Telephone Number
Franklin Federal Money Fund	$500/100	$100	800-227-6781
Fund for Government Investors, Inc.	$2500/none	$500	202-861-1800 (call collect)
Government Investors Trust	$2000/none	no minimum but $5 service charge on checks below $500	800-336-3063
Hilliard Lyons Government Fund, Inc.	$3000/500	$250	no toll-free number— 502-588-8400
Kemper Government Money Market Fund, Inc.	$1000/100	$500	800-621-1048
Lehman Government Fund, Inc.	$2500/100	$500	800-221-5350
Midwest Income Trust—Short Term Government Fund	$1000/50	$250	800-543-8721
T. Rowe Price U.S. Treasury Money Fund, Inc.	$1000/100	$500	800-638-5660
The Reserve Fund Inc.— Government Portfolio	$1000/1000	$500	800-223-5547
Scudder Government Money Fund	$1000/none	$500	800-225-2470
Vanguard Money Market Trust— Federal Portfolio	$1000/100	$250	800-523-7025

TABLE D
SELECTED TAX-FREE MONEY MARKET FUNDS WITH MORE THAN $100 MILLION IN ASSETS

Name	Minimum Initial Investment/ Subsequent Investment	Check-writing Minimum	Toll-free Telephone Number
Calvert Tax-free Reserves—Money Market Portfolio	$2000/250	$250	800-368-2748
Chancellor Tax-free Money Fund	$2500/500	$500	800-221-7984
Dean Witter/Sears Tax-free Daily Income Fund	$5000/100	$500	800-221-2685
Dreyfus Tax-exempt Money Market Fund, Inc.	$5000/100	$500	800-645-6561
Fidelity Tax-exempt Money Market Trust	$10,000/500	$500	800-225-6190
Municipal Cash Reserve Management	$10,000/1000	$500	212-742-6003 (call collect)
Nuveen Tax-exempt Money Market Fund, Inc.	$25,000/500	no checks	800-621-2431
Scudder Tax-free Money Fund	$1000/none	$500	800-225-2470
SteinRoe Tax-exempt Money Fund, Inc.	$2500/100	$100	800-621-0320
The Tax-free Money Fund	$5000/100	$500	800-223-7078
Vanguard Municipal Bond Fund— Money Market Portfolio	$3000/50	$500	800-523-7025

TABLE E
SELECTED MONEY MARKET FUNDS THAT BELONG TO A LARGER NO-LOAD FUND GROUP

Money Market Fund	Group Name	Toll-free Telephone Number
Alliance Capital Reserves, Inc.	Alliance Capital Management Corporation (subsidiary of Donaldson, Lufkin & Jenrette)	800-221-9513
Dreyfus Liquid Assets, Inc.	The Dreyfus Corporation	800-645-6561
Fidelity Cash Reserves	Fidelity Management & Research Co.	800-225-6190
Financial Daily Income Shares, Inc.	Financial Programs Inc.	800-525-9831
Lehman Cash Management Fund, Inc.	Lehman Management Co., Inc.	800-221-5350
Rowe Price Prime Reserve Fund, Inc.	T. Rowe Price Associates, Inc.	800-638-5660
Scudder Cash Investment Trust	Scudder, Stevens & Clark	800-225-2470
SteinRoe Cash Reserves, Inc.	Stein, Roe & Farnham	800-621-0320
The Value Line Cash Fund, Inc.	Value Line Group (Arnold Bernhard & Co.)	800-223-0818
Vanguard Money Market Trust— Prime Portfolio	Vanguard Group	800-523-7025

TABLE F
SELECTED LARGER GENERAL PURPOSE MONEY MARKET FUNDS WITH MORE THAN $500 MILLION IN ASSETS

Name	Minimum Initial Investment/ Subsequent Investment	Check-writing Minimum	Toll-free Telephone Number
Alliance Capital Reserves	$1000/$100	$500	800-221-9513
Cash Equivalent Fund, Inc. Money Market Portfolio	$1000/100	$500	800-621-1048
Cash Management Trust of America	$5000/50	$500	800-421-8791
Current Interest Money Market Fund	$1000/50	$500	713-751-2400 (call collect)
DBL Cash Fund—Money Market Portfolio	$1000/100	$500	800-272-2700
Delaware Cash Reserve, Inc.	$1000/25	$500	800-523-4640
Dreyfus Liquid Assets	$2500/100	$500	800-645-6561
Fidelity Cash Reserves	$1000/250	$500	800-225-6190
Fidelity Daily Income	$10,000/500	no minimum	800-225-6190
Franklin Money Fund	$500/100	$100	800-227-6781
IDS Cash Management	$2000/100	$500	800-328-8300
Kemper Money Market Fund, Inc.	$1000/100	$500	800-621-1048
Lehman Cash Management	$2500/100	$500	800-221-5350

TABLE F (*Continued*)

Name	Minimum Initial Investment/ Subsequent Investment	Check-writing Minimum	Toll-free Telephone Number
Liquid Capital Income Trust	$1000/250	$100	800-321-2322
Mass Cash Management Trust	$1000/none	$500	no toll free number 617-423-3500
NEL Cash Management Trust— Money Market	$1000/none	$250	800-225-7670
National Liquid Reserves	$1000/100	$500	800-223-7078
Oppenheimer Money Market Fund, Inc.	$1000/25	$250	800-525-7040
Reserve Fund—Primary	$1000/1000	$500	800-223-5547
Scudder Cash Investment Trust	$1000/none	$500	800-225-2470
Sears Liquid Assets Trust	$5000/1000	$500	800-932-0673
SteinRoe Cash Reserves	$2500/100	$100	800-621-0320
T. Rowe Price Prime Reserve	$1000/100	$500	800-638-5660
Vanguard Money Market Trust— Prime Portfolio	$1000/100	$250	800-523-7025

TABLE G
DOUBLE TAX-FREE MONEY MARKET FUNDS

Fund	Telephone
California	
Benham Cal. Tax-free Trust	800-472-3389
Shearson Lehman/Amer. Express Cal. Money Fund	through Shearson
Massachusetts	
Boston Co. Mass. Tax-free Money Fund	617-956-9748
Fidelity Mass. Tax-free Money Market Portfolio	800-225-6190
New York	
Reserve N.Y. Tax-exempt Trust*	800-223-5547
Shearson Lehman/Amer. Express N.Y. Money Fund*	through Shearson

*Triple tax-free, i.e., exempt also from N.Y. City income tax.

TABLE H
TAX-FREE YIELDS AND
THEIR TAXABLE EQUIVALENTS

Tax-free Yield (%)	Income Tax Bracket				
	30%	34%	38%	42%	48%
	Taxable Equivalent Yield (%)				
4.0	5.7	6.1	6.5	6.9	7.7
5.0	7.1	7.6	8.1	8.6	9.6
6.0	8.6	9.1	9.7	10.3	11.5
7.0	10.0	10.6	11.3	12.1	13.5
8.0	11.4	12.1	12.9	13.8	15.4
9.0	12.9	13.6	14.5	15.5	17.3
10.0	14.3	15.2	16.1	17.2	19.2
11.0	15.7	16.7	17.7	19.0	21.2
12.0	17.1	18.2	19.4	20.7	23.1

TABLE J

CONVERTING CURRENT (7-DAY) YIELDS INTO EFFECTIVE ANNUAL YIELDS

Current Yield (Uncompounded—%)	Equivalent Effective Annual Yield (Compounded Daily—%)
3	3.05
4	4.08
5	5.13
6	6.18
7	7.25
8	8.33
9	9.42
10	10.52
11	11.63
12	12.75
13	13.88
14	15.02
15	16.18
16	17.35
17	18.53
18	19.72
19	20.92
20	22.13

Arnold Corrigan, noted financial expert, is a senior officer of a large New York investment advisory firm. He holds bachelor's and master's degrees in economics from Harvard and has written for *Barron's* and other financial publications. He is the author of *How Your IRA Can Make You a Millionaire*.

Phyllis C. Kaufman is an entertainment lawyer and theatrical producer with degrees from Brandeis and Temple universities. Also a marketing and public relations consultant, she hopes that the NO-NONSENSE FINANCIAL GUIDES will help others conquer their "fear of finance."